Making Work Easy

Written by Rod Rees

Series Consultant: Linda Hoyt

WorldWise
Content-based Learning

Contents

I want a turn on the lever!

Introduction

Some things are very heavy. How do people move them?

Some things are up very high. How do people reach them?

We use pulleys and levers to move things that are heavy and reach things that are up high.

They make hard work easier.

Chapter 1

What is a pulley?

A pulley is made up of a **wheel** and a rope or **chain**. There is a groove in the wheel. The rope or chain fits into the groove.

If heavy things need to be moved, they can be attached to one end of the rope. When the other end of the rope is pulled, the wheel moves and helps to lift the load.

Pulleys help people move loads up, down or sideways. They help make moving heavy things easier.

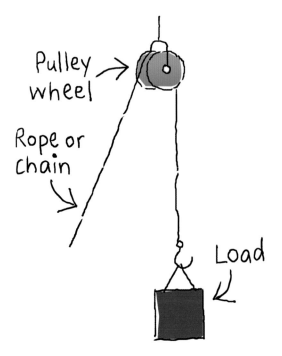

Pulley wheel

Rope or chain

Load

Pull on rope

Load is lifte

↑

Using pulleys

How do people move up and down
the outside of tall buildings?

People who clean windows and repair the outside of tall buildings
have very dangerous jobs. To stay safe, they wear a **safety harness**
that is attached to a rope that runs over a pulley at the top of the
building. When the worker pulls down on one end of the rope, the
pulley helps the worker move up and down.

How do rock climbers stay safe?

Rock climbers also wear a safety harness. People who are learning to climb inside on climbing walls wear a safety harness, too.

The harness is attached to one end of a rope. The rope runs over a pulley at the top of the rock climbing wall. Someone standing on the ground holds the other end of the rope. If the rock climber slips, the pulley makes it easy for the person on the ground to pull on the rope to stop the climber from falling.

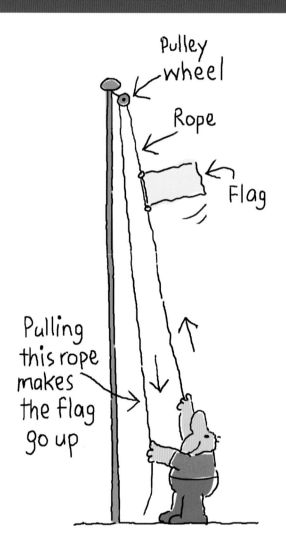

Pulley wheel

Rope

Flag

Pulling this rope makes the flag go up

How do you get a flag to the top of a flagpole?

A flagpole has a pulley at the top of the pole, where a rope runs over the pulley wheel. The flag is attached to the rope. When the rope is pulled, the flag can be moved up or down the flagpole.

How do you raise and lower sails on a yacht?

Pulleys are also used to raise and lower sails. The sails are attached to ropes that run over pulley wheels. By pulling on the ropes, the sails can be raised or lowered.

Chapter 2

What is a lever?

A lever is a bar or rod.

A lever can be pushed down or pulled up to help lift and move things. A longer lever makes it easier to move heavy objects.

Levers help people to move things that are heavy or difficult to lift.

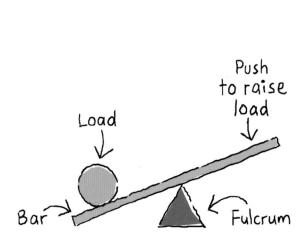

A lever

I want a turn on the lever!

A seesaw is a lever.

Using levers

How do you get the cap off a bottle?

People use **bottle openers** to remove bottle caps.

A bottle opener is a lever. By pulling up one end of the bottle opener, it is easy to lift off the bottle cap.

How do scissors work to cut paper or fabric?

Scissors are two levers joined in the middle. When someone squeezes the handles of the scissors together, the scissors will cut.

How do people move heavy boxes or furniture?

People use **trolleys** to move heavy boxes or furniture. A trolley is a lever. The longer the handles of the trolley, the easier it is to lift a heavy load. The **wheels** make it easier to move the load.

How do people move things around in a garden?

People use **wheelbarrows** to move sand, soil, plants in pots or rocks. The handles of the wheelbarrow are levers. The levers make it easier to lift things in a wheelbarrow, and the wheel makes it easier to move things around.

Chapter 3

Using pulleys and levers

How do people move heavy boxes on and off a ship?

People use **cranes** to move heavy loads on and off ships. Cranes have pulleys and levers. When a load is attached to the pulley, the load can be moved up and down. The arm of the crane is a lever. It can move the load up and down or from side to side.

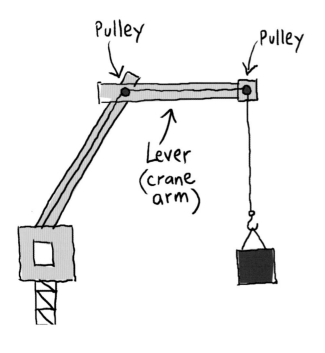

Pulley

Pulley

Lever (crane arm)

Conclusion

Pulleys and levers are used to lift and move things. People use pulleys and levers every day to make lifting heavy loads easier.

Glossary

bottle openers   tools used to take the caps off bottles

chain   a series of metal loops that are linked together

cranes   large machines used to reach and move things

trolleys   small carts pushed by a person

wheel   a hard round object that can turn and spin

wheelbarrows   tools used to move garden and building materials

Index

Pull on rope

Load is lifted